Small Group Workbook

Heard

The Power and Promise
of Christian Prayer

Dale Van Steenis
with Greg Smith

Black Lake Press
TELL YOUR STORY
BLACKLAKEPRESS.COM

Black Lake Press

TELL YOUR STORY
BLACKLAKEPRESS.COM

Cover design by Greg Smith of Black Lake Studio.

Published by Black Lake Press of Holland, Michigan.
Black Lake Press is a division of Black Lake Studio, LLC.
Direct inquiries to Black Lake Press at *www.blacklakepress.com*.

ISBN 978-0-9839602-1-8

contact the author directly through his website:
www.leadershipstrategies.org

Table of Contents

Session 1
"Why We Pray"

Read Chapter 1: "Why Wouldn't We?"

Why do we need to be convinced to pray?

We don't do anything unless we are presented with good reasons, so it's tempting to start a book about prayer by listing all the reasons that we ought to pray. Instead, I'd like to start with a simple question: why *wouldn't* we pray?

If we are followers of Jesus, then prayer is as much a basic part of our existence as _____, _____ or _____. We don't need to be persuaded to do those things. The questions are only about where, what, when and how.

Why should it be otherwise with prayer? As Christ-followers, do we need to be persuaded to pray at all? We can and should talk about methods and and strategies, but we shouldn't need to sell God's people on the idea that they ought to pray to him.

Is neglecting prayer a problem only for modern Christians? Why or why not?

- God's people have always tended to neglect prayer, long before the curses of our modern world. Can you think of some examples in the Bible when God's people neglected prayer? List them here:

- Why did they? How are we any different? Did the giving of the Holy Spirit at Pentecost make it harder to neglect God in prayer?

- How often do the the apostles urge the early Church to pray in their letters? If prayer came easily to Christians, would they need to be exhorted?

Why do Christians neglect their basic need to pray?

1. **They don't really _____ in _____.**

   - As Christians we *say* that prayer is the basic _____ of a _____ with its _____, and that through Christ's resurrection and the gift of the Spirit we have access to the throne of grace, but perhaps some of us don't really _____ it.

   - I "know" that prayer works because the Bible, pastors, and theologians tell me it does. But if I've never *experienced* _____ God in _____ it's hard for me to believe that it's necessary or beneficial. I'm not compelled to act.

- When did you first "meet" God in prayer, instead of just praying as an action? How old where you? What were the circumstances?

2. Sometimes we avoid prayer because we are _____ or _____ from God.

- Can you name some Bible characters who hid from or avoided God? Who? Why?

- Do we ever do the same thing?

3. Some of us pray, but we do all the _____.

- Sometimes our prayers become a tiresome one-way conversation, not because we are relentlessly petitioning him, but because we are trying not to let him get a word in edgewise. Why?

- What are we afraid he might say if we are quiet?

4. Sometimes we don't pray because of simple _____.

- Habits require effort. To lose weight, or to maintain an exercise program or household, we need discipline. How have you built positive habits into your prayer life?

5. Some people give up on prayer because they are angry about _____ _____. They don't believe that prayer "_____."

- Have you ever been angry or bitter toward God because he didn't answer your prayers in the way you wanted him to, or in the time frame you expected?

- Can you think of any Bible characters who became bitter toward God because they didn't think that he was responding to their prayers?

6. Some people don't know _____ to pray.

- How did Jesus teach us to pray?

- How did you learn to pray?

- Have you ever had any instruction in how to pray? Have you ever taught anyone?

7. Some Christians don't pray as a result of _____ _____.

- Why does Satan not want us to pray?

- What means does he use to prevent us from praying?

- How can we overcome Satan's efforts to thwart our prayers?

What happens when we neglect prayer?

- Regardless of the reasons why we don't pray, the bottom line is that many Christians are not so much neglecting a duty, but a _____ _____ of their existence.

- Just as insomniacs, anorexics, or thirsty persons who neglect to hydrate aren't so much disobedient as foolish, so those who neglect prayer are depriving themselves of ____ itself.

"Mother Theresa, when you pray, what do you say to God?"

- When Dan Rather interviewed Mother Theresa, how did she answer this question?

- Have you ever experienced this type of prayer? When did you first? How often do your prayers take this form?

- How can we cultivate this sort of familiarity with God?

Read Chapter 2: "It's What We Do"

While people of all religions "pray," it is what they imagine prayer to be that's different. For the Christian, prayer is fundamentally *a relationship with God.* It is not just offering praise, or confessing sin, or giving thanks, or bringing requests. All of those things are what we do *within* Christian prayer, but they aren't what prayer *is.* Nor are they ultimately the point of it. God doesn't want his people to pray because he needs to hear them say nice things about him. God doesn't need to be told what they did wrong (he already knows), or what they think that they want or need (he knows better than they do). God longs for people to be in intimate relationship with him. He longs for them to weave him into their lives.

God is our Father, and he longs for us to reach out to him for _____ and _____.

- Dale Van Steenis tells a story about a friend whose daughter recently graduated and moved away to another city, and a phone call that she made, which meant the world to him.

- Why did his daughter's call mean so much to the father?

- Why had she neglected calling him for so long?

The most basic thing that Christians do is to try to live in _____ _____ with Christ with the help of the Holy Spirit.

- All other aspects of the Christian life flow from us being children in _____ _____ with our Father (1 John 3:1).

- The Gospel is the story of how this relationship got broken and was restored. Using your own words, describe the Gospel as the story of a broken relationship.

- This is the heart of the Gospel: our Father longs to welcome us back into the intimate fellowship of the family. He has made that possible through the _____ and _____ _____.

The first formative experience for God's people: intimate fellowship with God is what we did in _____ before the ____ into ____.

- Describe Adam and Eve's intimate fellowship with God. How is that different than how we live today?

- After they sinned, how did that relationship change? What did they do?

- There was nothing preventing their intimate fellowship with him. It was how mankind was meant to live.

- Adam and Eve demonstrate what has shipwrecked the prayer lives of countless numbers of their descendants: _____ and _____ lead to _____. Why don't we want to talk to God sometimes?

The second formative experience for God's people: their journey through _____ _____with _____.

- The point was to teach them to _____ God into the _____ of their daily lives.

- They learned God's name. How? What significance does his name have for us?

- How did God teach Moses and the Israelites to live in his presence during the years in the desert?

The third formative experience for God's people: the _____ lived with _____ for three years.

- What does the incarnation teach us about prayer?

- For the better part of three years _____ became as much a part of their lives as their _____, _____, or _____.

- They were so comfortable that they were their real selves in front of him. Are you comfortable being your real self in front of God in prayer?

The fourth formative experience for God's people: the _____ Church.

- Why is it not a coincidence that it began in _____. Describe how, and why that is important.

- In their _____ to the early Church, the _____ share their vision and desire for the Christians to open their lives to intimate relationship with the Lord.

- Read: 1 Peter 2:5 and Romans 8:26. Do you experience this sort of ongoing (often non-verbal) conversation that God wants to have with us?

The future experience of God's people: in heaven, God _____ with his people.

- What is restored in heaven?

- This future intimacy in prayer isn't formative, it's _____. Why?

- How does the anticipation of fellowship with God in heaven transform our present lives?

Session 2
"Growing in Prayer"

Read Chapter 3: "For the Prize"

An allegory of Christian prayer.

Read the allegory of the large, upside-down cone.

The first time that you climb up to the next level, you realize three things:

1. God has _____ your _____.

   - That thing that you wanted up in this level has somehow been _____ _____ ____.

   - Maybe not exactly in the way that you expected or even asked for it to be

resolved, but you have _____ and
_____ that God has _____ the
_____ in the best way possible.

- You are _____.

- Early in your Christian life, did prayer
  seem like this? How easy was it to pray as
  a new Christian?

2. You're now in a _____ _____ than you
   were in the _____ _____.

   - There's more room to move around. Also,
     the walls of the cone are just a tiny bit
     more translucent, and just a tiny bit of
     light comes through them. You can
     almost see the outline of your hand if you
     hold it up in front of you.

3. Something else you _____ is just above
   you, through another round _____ in
   the ceiling over your head.

- Since prayer worked last time, you decide to _____ _____.

- How did God answering one of your prayers give you confidence to pray more?

When you pray again and climb to the next level, you realize several things:

- The space is _____ and _____ as you go higher up and deeper into the cone.

- You feel _____ and _____, knowing that he is in control of that situation.

- There's _____ _____ on this level. You hear a voice, and in the dim light you shuffle over and find _____ _____.

- You discover that you have some mutual concern, something that both of you need or want, and that it is probably overhead, through the opening in the ceiling above. Based on your previous experiences, you agree to _____ for it _____. The Holy Spirit gives you the _____ and _____ to climb upward into the unknown.

- Again, you come into a _____, _____ place.

- The higher up and deeper into God's Kingdom we go, the _____ and _____ it gets.

- As we begin our journey, what are we compelled by? How do these compulsions prompt us to pray?

- Read Psalm 37:7-8 and Psalm 118:5 in the King James Version. How do these verses describe the freedom God gives his people when they pray?

- How do we meet others along the way? How do they help us to grow in prayer?

- Read Hebrews 12:22-23. How does the cloud of witnesses help our prayer life?

- Seeing evidence of God's sovereignty makes us more _____ in him, and we become less concerned with our _____ and _____ because we know that he will _____ them all.

Early in the Christian life, prayer gets us out of _____, _____ places. As we mature in the Christian life, prayer takes us closer to "the _____."

- Read: 1 Corinthians 9:24, 9:27, Philippians 3:14, and Colossians 2:18.

- What do you think is "the prize?" What are you trying to gain in life, especially the spiritual life?

- What does Dale Van Steenis suspect that the prize is?

- Read Philippians 4:6-7. What do those who pray gain?

Read Chapter 4: "Ask, Seek, Knock"

The two most extensive of Jesus' monologues in the New Testament are found in Matthew chapters 5 through 7, and John: 13-17. Both contain much teaching about prayer (secret, humble, and quiet), fasting and prayer, patterns of prayer, and how to request help from the Father. A relationship with the Father was one method Jesus taught to secure answers to prayer. John 16:23 says, "If you ask the Father for anything, he will give it to you in My name." John 15:7 promises, "If you abide in Me, and My words abide in you, ask whatever you wish, and it shall be done for you."

On the human side of the prayer equation, we are called upon to do two things.

- First, God insists that our _____ be _____ to him.

- Second, that we ____, or make _____.

- How well do your prayers match this pattern?

Read Hebrews 5:7and Philippians 4:5-6.

- In Hebrews 5:7, we read that Jesus made prayers with "loud _____ and _____" and he "was _____." Why did Jesus pray that way?

- Was there a connection between how Jesus prayed and the result, as described in this verse?

- Do we pray the way Jesus did? Do you? Why or why not?

- In Philippians 4:5-6, Paul encourages petitioning the Father. Why is it unfortunate that when the verse numbers were added to the text, it divided the last part of verse 5 and verse 6? What is the connection between those two sentences? How is verse 6 logically connected with the last sentence in verse 5?

- Why does seeing connecting 5(b) with verse 6 give us encouragement? How does it change the way we pray?

Asking Prayer

- Asking prayer constitutes more than _____ percent of all praying. We have needs, and we ask God for help. This type of prayer is centered in things that touch us personally.

- What is the danger of asking prayer? It tends to become ____ _____. Do you observe this tendency in your asking prayers?

- All believers have this right in prayer and are encouraged to ask. However, to become a mature pray-er, one must grow in _____, engage in _____ _____, pray for _____ to be sent, and for the _____ of Jerusalem, etc. How do or could you cultivate these habits into your prayer life?

- We must also ultimately learn to pray "____ ____ be _____."

- God does not answer petitions that seek nothing more than to satisfy self-indulgent passions and personal aggrandizement. By _____ his word, _____ of sin, and _____ properly, our minds and spirits are much more _____ in weighing those things that we ask of him.

- In the average prayer meeting, a considerable amount of time is spent asking for help for matters that, if answered, would make life a little more _____ but which are relatively _____ when measured in the light of eternity. How can we keep our prayer meetings from falling into this habit?

- One measuring device to determine the quality of our requests is to ask the question: is the _____ of _____ being served? Who should ask this question when we pray together? How do we answer it? What should we do if it is not?

- Prayer that changes people and nations is of a _____ kind. Thankfully there are people who pray beyond _____ _____ and consider God's will before anything else. How can we become those kinds of people? How do we encourage them in our church?

Seeking prayer

- Asking prayer looks for answers to _____ requests. Seeking prayer searches primarily for _____, for _____, or _____. It searches for those facts that will answer a life-related _____, to discover that which will bring a _____ or _____.
- Obedient, patient seeking of the Lord will bring any honest _____ to a place of _____ with God. He reveals himself to the _____ seeker.

- Integrity of _____, persistent _____, and _____ are all requirements for our prayers to be answered. God adds another when he says, "_____ my face."
- What will be the end of a _____ and _____ search for God? *The true seeker will find him.* There are answers that need to be _____, petitions that need _____, truth to _____, _____ to engage, and an on-going _____ to build in seeking prayer.
- How often do you practice seeking prayer? What percentage, on average, of your prayer time is devoted to seeking prayer?

- In your church or small group prayer meetings, what percentage of the time is devoted to seeking prayer? Is that enough? If not, what can be done to encourage seeking prayer?

Knocking prayer

- The knocking prayer is prayer that seeks to _____ that which is _____. It refuses to take "no" for an answer. It discerns _____ and stands against it _____.

- Read Acts 12, and explain how it is an example of knocking prayer.

- Prayer is always _____ with God. It goes far beyond telling God things he _____ _____. The prayer of knocking is one that continues in _____ and _____ until there is a _____ from God.

Resistance

- What do you do when you "hit the wall" of resistance in prayer? Quit? Doubt? Pray once more and abandon the cause? Capitulate and let Satan triumph?

- Check your heart _____. Why are you praying what you are praying? Is there potential for God to _____ _____ from your prayer? Is your heart clean before him?

- Answers can be blocked by _____ sin.

- Are you praying according to the will of God? Are you asking him rightly or amiss?

- Have you discerned what kind of resistance you are encountering? Is it a demon, the flesh, or people? Are you in spiritual warfare?

Timing and Circumstances

- After one has determined the will of God in a prayer petition, the final matter in getting an answer relates to _____ and _____.

- When an intercessor encounters resistance in prayer, it is vital that he/she _____ the _____. Intercession is not the business of _____. In due season, that which has been _____ and _____ to you will be fully opened.

- Are you presently encountering resistance in prayer over a particular petition or question? How does it make you feel? How are you reacting to it?

- How can you encourage others in your life who are perhaps less experienced in prayer to stay the course and be patient for the blocks to be removed?

Session 3
"Persistence in Prayer"

Read Chapter 10: "Praying in the Face of Rejection"

The Story of Mrs. Smith

- Mrs. Smith was one of those intercessors who demonstrated great _____ in the midst of _____ and remained unrelenting in pursuit of an _____ from God. Like many others before her she prayed in the face of genuine _____ for years, and "through faith and patience inherit[ed] what [had] been promised" (Hebrews 6:12).

- What words did Mrs. Smith hear when she walked into the hospital room after her estranged husband's diagnosis? What did he ask her to do? How did she respond? Could you respond like Mrs. Smith were you in her place?

- Could you walk victoriously while living in such circumstances? Could you keep your anger and broken heart in check to the point that weeping prayer could still be made for an unfaithful spouse? Could you have stayed the course until a breakthrough came?

- Read Luke 18:1-8. How was she like Mrs. Smith?

- Had she or Mrs. Smith been rejected by God, despite the long wait for answer to their prayers? God was watching their _____ and listening to their _____. Read Psalms 30:5. Have you ever experienced that sort of a "night," and that sort of a "morning?"

- Have you ever felt what the widow inevitably felt? Have you felt absolutely alone in your prayer times? Have your circumstances screamed back at you when no immediate answer to prayer arrived at the time you needed it? Have you ever thought or said, "No one really understands or cares, and there is probably no help for my situation?"

- What is one of prayer's highest obstacles and most frequent enemies? The sense of _____ and _____.

- Jesus said, "At all times, they ought to pray" (Luke 18:1). That is a high standard. How can we pray at all times? Is it impossible to follow the example established by Jesus himself?

- Read 1 Thessalonians 5:15-17. It teaches us that we should, "Not repay _____ for _____," "_____ always," and, "Pray without _____."

- We ought to pray "at all times." At all times! Pray _____! Keep praying even when you _____ nothing, _____ nothing, and _____ nothing in response.

- How can a believer expect to secure lasting help in a flawed and fallen culture? It's simple: _____, _____-_____, _____ prayer.

The Timing of Answers to Prayer

- For reasons that God alone knows and controls, there are often delays–at times, long ones–in receiving answers to prayer. There are delays when you "_____" have a right to an answer and delays when all human _____ have been met, and even delays when the _____ is correct and the request is clearly within the will of God.

- Delayed answers are especially troublesome when you have an active _____. This _____ may or may not be another person. It can be a troublesome _____ you are facing, a _____ to be made, or perhaps an _____ _____. How long can you wait, then, for an answer?

- Faith and patience! These are terms that expose our character before they touch our needs. Faith is the _____ of _____ towards God; patience is the _____ _____that accepts long-suffering and quiet waiting.

- Faith has two environments in which it grows well. First, it grows by reading and hearing _____ _____. Secondly, faith is nurtured in effective _____ which increases our ability to exercise faith and belief that God will _____. He is _____ and he will _____.

Read Chapter 17: "The Great Rewards of Hanging Tough"

The Story of the Msangali Crusade.

- What had the American missionary fasted and prayed about? What questions did he want God to answer? Have you ever prayed those same questions? Have you gotten an answer?

- What mental picture did he receive? How did he respond to this vision? Has God ever given you a mental image without explanation?

- What reasons did he have to not go to Msangali when he learned where it was? Had God given him clear and direct instructions about what he should do? Has God ever given you vague directions that you had good reasons to not follow?

- Whose prayers were the crusade in Msangali an answer to? The missionary or the seven ladies? Did God direct both of them to pray as they did, knowing how he would bring a glorious answer?

The Story of Hannah

- This story is of another lady who prayed
  _____. How long had she prayed
  before God answered?

- If you have prayed a long time about a
  matter and have not, as yet, received an
  answer, you will understand intimately
  Hannah's pain, frustration and agony. Her
  story is a revelation regarding the process of
  long-term, repetitive praying, coupled with
  perseverance.

- Hannah's name means "God has
  _____ or _____." But there is
  more. Another word related to her name
  that helps us understand her as a person and
  intercessor is *canah*, which means "to
  _____ or _____ in kindness to an
  inferior." Another related term from the core
  of her name, *chnanah*, means "to pitch a
  tent, for abode or siege or _____ or war."
  In English we might say it this way, "I have

44

come with a goal and purpose in my heart, have put down a stake, and will not _____ until I ___ what I came for."

- Taken together, these words describe a God-possessed woman, full of destiny and purpose whose character was marked by _____, _____, and _____.

- Praying long term without a timely answer is genuinely _____ and can be _____ to our faith. The perception of our _____ becomes more intense when _____ turn into _____ of waiting for an answer. "Year after year" Hannah waited for an answer to her prayers.

- Prayer is often like war. Life becomes even more difficult when, in addition to the spiritual resistance in the heavenly realms, you are being treated _____ by those close to you. Read Psalm 57:4.

- Hannah's long-term praying affected her in positive ways. Her _____ increased, her _____ and _____ were tender before the Lord, and her _____ _____ increased exponentially because of persistent prayer

made during a season of personal
_____.

• What exactly is "bitter praying" and what can be learned from Hannah's experience?

• The term "distill" is used to describe Hannah's praying. The repeated nature of her prayers caused her motives to be _____ and her praying more _____ as she prayed year after year.

• Lou Engle says, "The task of prayer is to get our _____ _____ with his." How do we know if and when our hearts are aligned with his? What active steps can we bring them into line?

- One of the great keys in getting prayer answered is to be in _____ with God's eternal _____. How can we indicate that we are in agreement? How do we overcome our own resistance if we are not in agreement with what we perceive to be God's purposes?

- The lonely, agonizing hours of prayer are the process God uses to _____ our motives and _____ our hearts with his. It takes time to _____ the pure things God wants.

- What are some ways that God has distilled your heart through prayer? Has God ever used a particular issue in your life to purify and align you with him?

Session 4
"Mobilizing the Church"

Read Chapter 8: "The Prayer Gathering"

The largest prayer mobilization in church history is now in progress. If the actual number of people praying were counted, that number would be the highest in history. Inestimable good is being done through multiple prayer efforts and much more will follow because God loves prayer and praying brings divine rewards.

Prayer meetings are back! They can be wonderful, alive, and effective if the leaders are trained in the specifics of handling and creating good meetings. They can be positive and meaningful if there is a high level of participation in the meetings themselves. They can be attractive if you advertise what God has done as a result of intercession. And they can be faith building from on-going testimonials. Let's get praying!

Personal Prayer

- Discipline, as well as a _____ and _____ are required to grow a successful prayer life. If we do not have a specific _____ and _____, we probably will not pray regularly or effectively.

- The following is a simple guide you can use every day and almost anywhere to develop structure in your personal prayer time.

  - Open with _____.

  - Read scriptures _____ and _____ (more for meaning than quantity).

  - Ask for _____.

  - Ask _____ he wants you to pray.

  - Make _____ and _____.

  - Listen for God's _____.

- _____ _____ what you hear (obey _____ if God sends an order).

- Worship and _____ _____.

- Develop your prayer time until it becomes a life giving habit!

- How many of the practices listed above do you regularly incorporate into your prayer life?

- How do you discipline yourself for personal prayer?

- Do you have a regular schedule? A preferred location? What systems or accountability partners do you use to maintain your prayer routine?

- Has personal prayer of the type described above become an ingrained habit in your life?

- What sort of materials do you use, in addition to your Bible? There are many daily devotional guides in any Christian bookstore and in many secular ones as well. Find one that works with you and for you. Use anything that will _____, _____, _____ and _____ your prayer time.

Corporate Prayer Gatherings

- There are many types of corporate prayer gatherings, including prayer _____, _____, days of _____ and _____, and national and local days of prayer.

- Strength comes in _____. Does your church participate with any organizations or programs to mobilize large-group prayer nationally or internationally?

- Lively, well-led, _____-_____, corporate intercessory gatherings are much needed. Prayer gatherings express _____ upon God.

- Unfortunately, there are genuine enemies of corporate prayer gatherings. The big three are

  1. _____ _____.

  2. _____.

  3. Excessive _____ _____.

  These challenges also affect one's personal prayer life along with one giant enemy– _____!

Sleep and Its Antidote. How can you conquer the sleep problem?

- Read the story about the man who fell asleep in the all-night prayer meeting.

- _____ _____ to pray.

- _____ back and forth.

- By _____ and _____, your body requires more oxygen. Walking deepens breathing and circulation and this stimulates _____.

Talking and Protracted Need Sharing

- Talking and extensive need sharing are negatives that seriously _____ the power and _____ of a prayer gathering.

- The verbalization of prayer needs at the beginning of a meeting _____ faith.

- It is appropriate and needful to make our requests known to God. However, these needs should not become the _____ of a prayer time. _____ must always be the _____.

• When your mind is loaded with needs before it is _____ on _____, it will be hard to pray in a faith-filled, effective way.

• Start with a _____ or two and then have a time of hearty _____. You could add a _____ of recently answered prayer. Then, when there is a _____ _____ of God being present, that is the time to lift requests to God.

• After a lengthy _____ in God's _____, making petitions is an easy matter.

Selfish Praying

• Furthermore, our prayers need to be centered in, "___ _____ come [and] ____ ____ be _____."

• As mentioned in Chapter 4, start by asking God _____ to pray about a matter. Praying God's _____ and praying with _____ is the starting point of effective praying. It will lift us from the zone of ____-_____, personal _____ to _____ the things important to God.

Wandering Thoughts

- There are few points at which the thoughts tend to be more non-_____ and wander further into a mental ___-_____-_____ than at the point of prayer. The "_____" part of man (mind, emotions, will) has the capacity to engage in innumerable _____ _____ simultaneously.

- Several things can be done to help concentration:

  1. Pray _____.

  2. Pray the _____ of _____.

  3. Stay with steps one and two until you have a keen and clear conscious _____ of God's _____. Then you can _____ requests easily.

Leadership

- Local prayer gatherings need leaders with _____ _____ to guide prayer meetings.

- These services should never be _____ by one or two people or by the _____ of one or two. They must be conducted by a person led by the Holy Spirit and must not be _____ or _____.

- The leader must be able to discern "where" a meeting __ and "where" it _____ be _____.

- Prayer leaders must be _____ and _____. They must keep _____ on everything said and done. Prayer leaders must be _____ and periodically monitored for _____.

- _____ _____ Christians are needed in this position since prayer and intercession are the jugular of the church.

Making it All Come Together

- What is the best kind of prayer service? It is the one that _____ in your _____, the one in which the people are _____ with the _____, the one in which everyone can _____ _____, and the one in which the people _____ _____ God. Nothing else is really important!

- All the modes mentioned above and dozens more are needed at one time or another. _____ prayer concerns must, of necessity, be mingled with _____ requests and needs into which the entire prayer group can partner in intercession.

- A prayer group leader could facilitate thirty or forty minutes of _____ prayer followed by a few minutes of _____ requests handled on a one-by-one basis. By these means, the entire group can participate and add _____ by praying in _____.

Reality Check

- Every prayer event needs a periodic _____ _____. What happened as a result of our praying? It helps to keep a prayer log listing both _____ and _____ by date. Endless praying without confirmation of answers leads to _____ and _____. Make answered prayer a public matter. Let everyone know what God has done, especially those who prayed.

Questions:

- Do the prayer meetings at your church or organization make good use of the practices mentioned above?

- What are the best things about your prayer meetings?

- What are the biggest obstacles keeping your prayer meetings from being more effective?

- If you are a leader, what can you do to improve your prayer meetings? If you are a participant, how can you help your leaders in their ministry?

Read Chapter 7: "About Intercessors"

- Intercessors are among the _____ _____ but _____ _____ persons in God's work. They are hard to ____, challenging to _____, and _____ to look after. They are _____ by God and have special _____ to remain _____ for years over important matters should that need be required.

- Because they feel just a bit of what God feels, they _____ very much—perhaps at times even in a _____ way—about the _____ of God. Intercessors are identified by the following characteristics:

  - *Intercessors pray on _____ of _____.* The "others" may be God or people because both have needs to fulfill.

  - *Intercessors are _____ and _____.* Tears and passion are marks that distinguish intercessors. A deep passion for God and _____ motivates them. Intercessors ____ before the _____ of God.

  - *Intercessors are _____.* It is the business of intercessors to hear God's voice and, from that hearing, to pray for his _____ to be accomplished. There is great value in having people in prayer ministries who are _____ to God's voice and who know how to _____ God's voice from the many that clamor for attention.

- *Intercessors are* _____ *and* _____. Warfare with demonic spirits is a part of intercession, and intercessors are not ones to shy away from a _____.

- *Intercessors are usually* _____ _____. There are two activities that invite attacks from hell more than any others. The first is _____. Soul winners are depopulating hell and populating heaven and the devil doesn't like it. The second activity that invites attack is _____. Why? Because, by its nature, intercession _____ evil in the spirit realm.

Intercessors and Congregational Life

- Intercessors need _____ and a _____ to pray beyond the normal flow of church services.

Separation from the main congregation is needed but, at the same time, pastors must ensure that _____ is resisted.

- Intercessors should not, and cannot, _____ a Sunday service for _____ purposes as these are typically for worship, teaching, and fellowship. However, intercessors play an important role in _____ the _____ for everything that happens in those public services.

- They pray for the meetings _____ they happen.

- Some churches have rotating teams that pray while the _____ is going on.

- During prayer times or at the ____ of a service, these persons are available for prayer, although that is a different level than _____ intercession.

Prophetic Intercessors

- Because intercessors are _____ about seeking God's face, they can–better than others–_____ the true nature of a thing being prayed for, as well as the potential solution. Many intercessors have a secondary gifting in the _____ realm.

• Those who intercede with prophetic anointings and those who lead them develop a grid of _____. They need a framework that allows information to come to the leadership to be processed as to _____, _____, and _____. The leadership needs to consider _____ and _____ to respond, and whether it is _____ to be shared with the _____.

Intercessors need refreshing and special attention

• Because of frequent attacks, intercessors need t i m e s   o f   _____   a n d _____.

• What do intercessors need?

    1. _____.

    2. _____.

    3. _____.

    4. _____.

5. _____.

6. A special _____ to pray. The best intercession is done away from crowds, even church crowds.

7. Intercessors also need _____ and _____ in their ability to hear and keep _____ information.

8. Also, intercessors themselves need _____. Church leaders need to keep the needs of the intercessors before the congregation.

Questions

• Does your church have recognized intercessors? Does your pastor or leaders make use of them in the ministry?

• Are you an intercessor? Do you play that role in your church? Does your pastor or leaders recognize you in that role?

• Does your church's intercessors have what they need to minister effectively through their calling? If not, what could be done to empower, equip and encourage them?

Session 5
"God's Will and Spiritual Warfare"

Read Chapter 16: "The God Who Hears and Responds."

How we ask for something depends on what we believe about the person we are asking. If we think they are inferior to us, or owe us something, we might be demanding. If we are speaking to someone we don't know well, but would like to impress, we might be formal and especially courteous. If we are asking a big favor of someone to whom we are in debt, we might be solicitous.

What does it reveal about who we think God is when we tell him that we only want something if he was going to do it anyway? Does it prove that we have a humble, polite, respectful, and deferential character? Or does it demonstrate what we believe about his character?

When God asks us what we want, he wants us to to be _____ and ____ him.

- How are we sometimes like dinner party guests when we pray?

- Why are we so hesitant to ask God for what we want? Is it genuine _____?

- What is the difference between sincerely praying for God's will and hedging our prayers to protect ourselves from being hurt?

- Do you ever tell God, "If it is your will..." because you are afraid you will be _____ if you tell him the truth?

Praying, "If it be your will..." can be motivated by _____ _____, or by a _____ of God's character.

- Read Matthew 25:24-25 (the Parable of the Talents). What makes the master most angry: that the servant didn't make a profit with the investment, or the _____? What did the _____ imply about the master?

- Read Matthew 7:9-10. How does our Father really feel about his children's requests?

- Does a loving father always give his children everything they ask for? Should that stop them from asking?

- Read Philippians 4:6-7. How should we ask for things in prayer?

- Read 2 Corinthians 12:8-9. How many times did Paul ask God to give him what he wanted? What was God's response?

In the Garden of Gethsemene Jesus asks God to "let this cup pass" if it is "_____."

- If we are supposed to express our desires to God, why does Jesus say, "Yet not what I _____, but as you _____?" (Mark 14:36)

- Jesus does share his human desire with the Father (he wishes there was some other _____to _____ God's plan), but his greatest _____ is for God's glory and our salvation.

Does God ever change his mind in _____ to our prayers?

- Read Exodus 32:9-14. What does God want to do to the Israelites?

- How does Moses reply to God's plan?

- In verse 14 tells us that, "The LORD _____ and did ___ _____ on his people the disaster he had threatened." Why did God change his mind?

We have a God who not only _____ us what we want, but who also _____ and _____.

- He won't accept our _____, _____, or false _____.

- He refuses to let us _____ _____ in prayer, not asking so that we won't risk being told no.

- He promises that if you will _____ with an open heart, he will do the same.

- Where might that take you? You'll have to tell him _____ you _____ to find out.

Read Chapter 9: "Spiritual Warfare and Intercession"

This chapter is short. Why?

- First, the Bible has little to show by _____ or say in _____ about the subject of spiritual warfare.

- Secondly, if God wanted us to be specialists in spiritual warfare, one could conclude that he would have made all that _____ in his _____.

- I do believe in a literal devil that has some _____ powers in the universe. What I struggle with is how much _____ and _____ he deserves in the context of our prayer lives.

- Soul _____ is the primary New Testament means to _____ Satan's efforts on planet earth. In that process people are taken from the Kingdom of _____ to the Kingdom of _____.

In the New Testament, there are only three places where warfare is mentioned. There is mention of warfare in the following texts:

- 1 Corinthians 9:7: The context speaks of soldiers who fight deserving ____.

- 1 Timothy 1:18: Paul instructs Timothy towards faithfulness and to war or to contend for the faith since some have _____ _____.

- 2 Corinthians 10:4: This verse speaks of weapons of war not being _____. The object of the fight rests in the struggles in one's _____ life.

- Demons are not mentioned in any of the above verses directly or by inference.

- Is Ephesians 6:11-20 about spiritual warfare as it is commonly imagined in contemporary Christian circles? These verses describe the _____ that believers have against demonic _____ and _____ which wage war in the heavenly realms. The context does not indicate in any way that believers should be on a _____ _____ against Satan.

- What does bring a change in a home, community and church? Praying people do! When people pray _____ and

_____ and then live out the life of God that flows from that in a Holy Spirit-directed and scripturally defined way, changes occur at every level.

• Communities are _____ when people are converted to Christ and _____, not before.

• In place of a demon and fortress mindset, let us ever be Jesus _____ and _____ about persevering prayer.

Session 6
"Even When God is Silent, He Always Hears"

Read Chapter 12: "When God is Silent"

Consider the hymn, *In the Garden,* by Charles Austin Miles. It's a beautiful image of what Christian prayer is like. Or is it what prayer is like _____? Or what prayer is _____ to be like? Or what we wish that it _____ be?

- Have you ever had a time when it felt like you waited in the garden, but that God didn't _____ up?

- Have you ever had a time when God seemed _____, like you've been talking to someone on the phone and the call got _____, while you kept talking?

- Have you ever prayed, waiting for some acknowledgement that God hears? Like you were waiting for an important phone call, or email, or letter?

- Have your prayers ever been coupled with _____, and you became distracted by your environment?

- Has prayer ever felt like a _____? Or like an awkward and strained _____?

Can Christians, filled with the Holy Spirit, ever fail to hear God's _____?

- How did Mother Theresa express her periodic doubts and seasons of silence from God in her personal letters? Have you ever felt the same way? What prompted them? What caused them to pass?

- In John Bunyan's Pilgrim's Progress, what is the name of the key that allows Christian to escape from the dungeon of Despair in Doubting Castle? How can you make use of this key when you feel doubt in your prayer life?

There are many reasons why God might seem silent in our prayer lives.

- One reason is "_____ _____." God may only seem silent because the rest of our life is too _____; all the other voices, distractions, stresses and thoughts running through our mind drown him out. God might be _____, but we might not be able to hear him until we turn down the volume on everything competing with his voice. How do you do that?

- Another reason is because the conversation is moving on his _____, not ours. What if what we think is silence is really just a _____? How do you learn patience in your prayer life?

- Sometimes God *has* spoken, but is waiting for us to _____ _____ what he said. Perhaps he wants us to _____ the last thing he told us to do before he gives us any new _____. Has God ever waited for you to catch up with him?

- Another reason God might seem silent is that he's forcing us to _____ ___. God gives the new Christian the sort of attention that a mother gives a new baby, but God is not content to let us remain spiritual _____ forever. God sometimes allows us to go through the dark night of the soul so that we can learn to not be afraid of the _____.

- I believe in the sun even when it isn't _____. I believe in love even when I do not ____ it. And I believe in God even when he is silent.

Read Chapter 13: "The Reception Room of Prayer"

Prayer is often an _____ exercise. Why?

- To a sophisticated person, it seems genuinely _____ to speak ____ ____ ____ as though speaking to someone near, when no one is _____. Have you ever felt this way? Have you ever felt ridiculed for praying?

- For Christians, prayer is neither _____ nor _____. Those who believe in Jesus Christ also believe his word that he will not and cannot _____. Have you ever doubted that God hears or cares about your prayers? How did you overcome that doubt?

- Christians accept the proposition that if God is sought after by means of prayer—in whatever _____, _____ or _____ state—it is on the basis that there is a benevolent God in heaven who can hear and who will respond. Have you ever avoided prayer because you couldn't do it the "right" way at that time?

Read Revelation 4 and 5.

- In Revelation 4, the point of view moves from earth to _____, from _____ to the churches in Asia to a specific focus on God's _____.

- God's _____ is where our prayers find _____ and _____. How does that make you feel about your prayers? Is it intimidating or liberating? Does it make you feel anxious or peaceful?

- Read Revelation 5:8. What were the twenty-four elders holding? What did these vessels contain?

- Revelation 5 reveals that God, on his throne, is concerned with his people's _____ and _____. Does our focus match his? Why or why not?

In many church cultures, praise times and prayer times are _____.

- Psalms 100:4 (KJV) says, "Enter into his gates with thanksgiving, and into his courts with praise." Praise is the _____ _____ for prayer.

- Why do some churches separate these two aspects of worship? Should they be? What do they have in common?

- What does it mean to say that praise and prayer times are two expressions of the same _____ anointing?

Read Daniel 9:20-23.

- Where and how was Daniel praying?

- How did God respond to Daniel's prayers?

- Encouragement is to be found here by all those who wonder if God really hears and listens, and when. This Scripture is clear about the _____ of God's response. When did God send Gabriel to Daniel?

- You were heard and responded to by the Father the _____ you prayed and *an angel is* _____ *to you now with your answer.*

- How long did it take for Gabriel to arrive? What delayed his arrival? If we don't see an immediate response to our prayers, does it mean that God hasn't begun responding?

Read Chapter 15: "How to Get Your Prayers Answered"

- Unanswered prayer is the chief complaint when the topic of prayer is openly discussed.

- _____, _____, and even _____ have been manifested in my presence by people who felt betrayed by God at their point of need.

- Praying _____, praying at the _____ _____ (if that's possible), and praying ____ of the ____ of God are valid reasons for him to withhold response. He always has _____ in mind

and his purposes cannot be _____
to meet what we might call an emergency in our
lives.

- Read Hebrews 5:7. It offers some major insights
  into the prayer life of Jesus. It tells us that, *"He
  was* _____." What a wonderful affirmation
  and encouragement to prayer! Those words are
  filled with _____ and _____. To be
  _____ and _____ is the goal of
  everyone who prays.

- At times, do you sense that that your prayers
  are like a rocket launch–full of fire and power
  and rapidly on their way into the heavens? You
  feel God's presence, praying is easy, and there
  seems to be little resistance from the devil. The
  assurance of an answer seems guaranteed. How
  often does prayer feel this way to you?

- But are there times when you feel your prayers
  do not get beyond the ceiling of the place where
  you are praying? Have you ever had that
  impression that your prayers did not get any

further than the tip of your tongue? Have you ever said prayers that–at least to the senses– drew no presence, experienced no warfare, and appeared to gain no ground?

- Jesus' experience was very different. We read that, "He was _____." Why was he heard? How did he pray to get a response? What method did he use in bringing his earthly concerns before the Father?

- He found it _____ to pray. Luke 5:16 tells us that, "But he himself would often slip away into the wilderness and pray." Notice the words _____, _____, and _____. Jesus was well acquainted with _____ and _____. His life pattern called him there often. If Jesus made going away to be alone in prayer a lifestyle, can any less be expected of us? Does your prayer pattern follow his example?

- He prayed with loud _____ and _____. Read John 11:1-47. Notice verse 33. It tells us that, "[Jesus] was deeply moved in _____ and _____." Before the tomb of Lazarus, Jesus _____.

- In John 11:40-42 (KJV), Jesus held a conversation with his Father. Interestingly, he did not ask for power to resurrect Lazarus. Instead, he praised his Father for _____ him. Ultimately, everyone who prays has one goal, to be _____ by God!

- Webster's dictionary defines crying as, "An _____ utterance of distress, pain or rage." Weeping and crying gives expression to the _____ and _____ feelings of the soul at a level where words are inadequate to convey the full weight of meaning. Pain and distress become compressed into the subconscious and the spirit of weeping gives expression. Crying provides _____.

- Recall the experience of Hannah as she was being observed by Eli the priest. In her heaviness, she poured out her heart before the

Lord. She "wept bitterly." When the soul is
_____, weeping gives
_____.

- The _____ of a person, the so-called inner man,
is the storage area for all the _____
activities of life. Day after day and year after
year, pain and joy, hurt and hilarity are
gathered in the souls and retained by the
memory, and wait for _____ and
_____.

He Could Have, But He Didn't

- Praying often centers in cries for
_____ from some distress or
_____ of some need.

- The greatest single challenge in prayer comes
from those days and hours when God seems to
be _____, _____, or otherwise
_____, removed and _____ from my
needs. Our mind says he is not there. Our soul
languishes in _____. Our emotions say
more prayer is not worth the _____; they
instruct me to stop trying to make God do

_____. Have you been near these circumstances at all?

- What can we do in those moments? Should we rely on only our emotions and intellect?

- In honor of his passion, Jesus prayed to the "one who was able" (Hebrews 5:7). That is the secret. *Prayer is made to a* _____, and not to a _____ _____, _____, or _____.

- Moses had to grip the revelation of the "I Am," the _____-_____ God.

- Daniel discovered his deliverance in the _____.

- Israel in its _____.

- Gideon in the _____.

- Paul on the _____ road.

- John on _____.

- To whom shall we flee when we are in need? "To the One who is _____." To fully understand the power of prayer, every believer must somewhere and sometime have an _____ with the _____ One. That

encounter must be wrapped in the
_____ and _____ of the Holy
Spirit.

- Since we know the Father is sovereign and can do as he pleases, why did he choose not to rescue his Son from the horrible death that was certainly ahead?

- Why would rescuing Jesus from his persecutors have not demonstrated God's love?

- How does Christ's death and resurrection demonstrate that the Father always answers prayers in the _____ of _____, and not to _____ our comfort level.

- Hebrews 5:7 also says Jesus was heard "because of his _____" (some translations say "because he _____ God.")

- That phrase is the key to understanding the entire verse and to answer the question, why Jesus' prayers were answered. The term "piety" in the original Bible language is *eulabeia,* which means _____ or _____.

- Taken to its roots, the term is from a combination of words that mean "good" and "to take hold of." It is used in the verb form and should be translated "moved with fear." To clarify understanding, the term embodies the idea of _____ for God, to take hold of God _____ and _____, to move in the reverential awe of God.

- The prayers of Jesus were answered because of the _____ of his _____:

  - He lived a _____ life.

  - He regarded his Father in every _____, _____, and ___, and lived his life under the _____ of the Father.

- In the western church today, sin is lightly regarded. There is little _____ of God and thus little aspiration towards _____. Thus, it is no wonder that our prayers are not answered.

To be "heard" we must become more Christ-like in our _____, _____, and _____ of God.

- Regardless of delays and deferrals, take solace in the fact that God is _____! Even though loud crying and tears may be your condition at the moment, he is still able to make a _____ in your life.

- As an exercise, and before you pray again, take a few minutes and enter into a worship mode before the living God who is able to deliver. He has promised that, "If any man be a worshipper of God, and doeth his will, him he heareth." (John 9:31 KJV).

About the Author

Dale Van Steenis received his spiritual formation in a large local church in the midwest. Since his family was heavily involved in the life of the church, he moved into leadership at an early age. From his mid-teens he has worked in ministry in music, speaking, missions, and youth pastorates. Pastorates have been served in Texas and California. he led a youth program serving more than 400 churches for five-and-a-half years. For the last twenty five years he has been the director of Leadership Strategies International (LSI) which has taken him to more than 100 nations. LSI is a ministry designed to train Third World ministers and church workers. Additionally, LSI assists thousands of people annually through humanitarian assistance programs such as medical assistance, food, water purification projects, and agricultural improvement programs. His humor, world wide experiences, hunger for renewal, and strong academic background combine to bring strength to church leaders worldwide.

Dale and his wife Gloria are parents of four children and reside in Southern California.

You may contact him through his website:
www.leadershipstrategies.org